Iguanas

By Sandra Donovan

Steadwell Books

Raintree Steck-Vaughn Publishers
A Harcourt Company

Austin · New York
www.raintreesteckvaughn.com

ANIMALS OF THE RAIN FOREST

Published by Raintree Steck-Vaughn Publishers,
an imprint of Steck-Vaughn Company.

Library of Congress Cataloging-in-Publication Data
ISBN 0-7398-5372-4
Printed and bound in the United States of America
1 2 3 4 5 6 7 8 9 10 WZ 05 04 03 02

Produced by Compass Books

Photo Acknowledgments
Digital Stock, cover; Root Resources/Earl Kubis, title page; Kenneth Fink, 23–29;
Roving Tortoise Productions/Tui De Roy, 6, 14, 16, 18, 21, 22; Visuals Unlimited/Ken
Lucas, 8; Beth Davidow, 11, 12; Joe McDonald, 24, 26.

Editor: Bryon Cahill
Consultant: Sean Dolan

Content Consultant
Robert Ehrig, International Iguana Society, Florida

This book supports the National Science Standards.

Contents

CENTRAL
AMERICA

Gulf of Mexico

VENEZUELA

*Pacific
Ocean*

COLOMBIA

GALAPAGOS
ISLANDS

ECUADOR

BRAZIL

PERU

Range of the
Marine Iguana

Surrounding
Land

BOLIVIA

Water

Borders

N
W E
S

CHILE

A Quick Look at Iguanas

What do iguanas look like?

Iguanas are lizards with long bodies that can reach up to 6 feet (2 m). They have four short, strong legs. An iguana's tail is usually twice as long as its body. An iguana is usually green, brown, gray, blue, or orange and may have stripes or patterns on its skin.

Where do iguanas live?

Iguanas live in warm parts of Central America, South America, the West Indies, the Galapagos Islands, Fiji, Mexico, and the southwestern part of the United States.

What do iguanas eat?

Iguanas eat soft leaves, flowers, and fruit. They get much of their water from their food and lick raindrops from leaves when they are thirsty.

This iguana is eating the last leaves from a rain forest tree branch.

Iguanas in the Rain Forest

Iguanas are lizards. Lizards are reptiles with four legs. Their long body and tail are covered with **scales**. Scales are small, thick, tough pieces of skin. A reptile is a crawling animal with a backbone. Reptiles breathe air and are also **cold-blooded**. The body of a cold-blooded animal warms or cools to about the same temperature as the air or water around it.

The scientific name for iguanas is *Iguanidae* (ee-GWAH-nuh-dee). This word means large lizard in the Spanish language.

Iguanas live in warm places like tropical forests and rain forests. A rain forest is a warm place where many different trees and plants grow close together, and a lot of rain falls. Iguanas eat fruits and berries. Then the seeds in their waste, or droppings, help more trees and plants to grow.

> This iguana is resting on a tree in the rain forest where it lives.

Where Do Iguanas Live?

Wild iguanas live only in warm parts of the world. Rain forest iguanas like the thick tropical forests of Central America, South America, Mexico, the West Indies, Figi, and the Galapagos (gah-LAP-ah-gohs) Islands.

Different kinds of iguanas are found in different **habitats**. A habitat is a place where an animal usually lives or a plant grows. Many iguanas live in the hot, wet rain forests, deserts, or dry tropical forests. Others live around the ocean.

Most iguanas are **arboreal**. This means they live in trees. Iguanas are very good climbers. They spend much of their time about 40 to 50 feet (12 to 15 m) above ground, in the **canopy**. A canopy is an area of thick leaves and branches high above the rain forest floor.

The canopy provides a place for iguanas to hide from predators. Predators are animals that hunt other animals and eat them. Iguanas are usually green, gray, brown, or black. Some have stripes or patterns on their skin. Their normal color camouflages them in the trees. **Camouflage** is colors, shapes, and patterns that help an animal blend in with its background.

Iguanas are good swimmers and usually live near water. Those that do not live by oceans make their homes by rivers and streams.

Many iguanas live in areas with other iguanas. Each iguana has its own territory. A **territorial** animal lives and looks for food in its territory. The iguana will often defend its territory from other iguanas.

Kinds of Iguana

There are 700 **species** of iguana. A species is a group of animals or plants that share common features and are closely related to each other. These species are broken down into larger groups. The three main groups of iguana are common iguanas, land iguanas, and marine, or water, iguanas.

Common iguanas, or green iguanas, live in the rain forests of Central America and South America. These are the biggest iguanas. They can grow to be more than 6 feet (180 cm) long. Their skin is green and gray.

Land iguanas live on the Galapagos Islands, off the coast of Ecuador in the Pacific Ocean. Land iguanas grow to be about 3 feet (91 cm) long. They have green, brown, and black coloring.

Marine iguanas also live on the Galapagos Islands. They live in the water around the islands. These green and brown iguanas are about 3 feet (91 cm) long. They are the only kind of lizard that can eat underwater.

This is a male common iguana.

   The Fiji iguana is a rare type of iguana. The iguanas belonging to this group are found only on the island of Fiji in the Pacific Ocean. They live mostly in rain forest trees. Fiji iguanas are green with white spots or with blue or white stripes. Some have yellow nostrils. They grow to about 2 feet (61 cm) long.

You can see the dewlap hanging from this iguana's neck.

What Do Iguanas Look Like?

Iguanas are different sizes. The smallest iguana, the Short-horned lizard, is only 4 inches (10 cm) long.

In other ways, most iguanas look alike. They all have scaly skin. Scales are made of a material called keratin. People's fingernails are also made of keratin. An iguana's scales help it hold moisture and heat within its body. Some iguanas have a row of spiky scales down their back, tail, or under their chin.

Iguanas may have a dewlap, too. The dewlap is a piece of colored skin on the throat. Males use their dewlap to attract mates and to appear larger in order to scare off enemies, such as wild dogs, cats, and larger iguanas.

Iguanas have a long head with three eyes. They have one eye on each side of their head. The third eye is on top of the head. This eye cannot be seen from the outside. Scientists think iguanas can see only light and dark with this third eye.

Iguanas all have a long body with four short, strong legs. Iguanas have five toes on each foot. The toes have long, sharp claws at the end. Iguanas use these claws to dig and to climb trees quickly.

An iguana's tail is usually twice as long as the rest of its body. An iguana's tail has many uses. Rain forest iguanas use their tails as weapons. They snap them at their enemies. They also use their tails to balance when they run. Iguanas swish their tails back and forth to swim. This tail movement helps push them through the water.

This land iguana is eating a flower.

What Iguanas Eat

Most wild iguanas eat flowers, leaves, and soft fruits. They are herbivores. An herbivore is an animal that eats only plants.

Adult common iguanas of the rain forest eat fruit, berries, and leaves. Young common iguanas may eat insects, too. The protein from the insects helps them grow. Marine iguanas eat seaweed found on rocks at the edge of the ocean.

Iguanas do not have to travel far to find food. They eat leaves and fruit from the trees they live in. They also gather food on the ground of the rain forest. They have very good senses of smell and sight, which make it easy to find food.

Iguanas get their water from the moist food they eat. Their body takes the moisture from their food and uses it. They also lick drops of rain from tree leaves.

This marine iguana is eating the seaweed off a rock.

Eating and Digesting Food

Once iguanas find their food, they use their long toes and claws to gather it. They bite and grind the food with their sharp teeth.

Iguanas sit in the sun after they eat. The warmth of the sun helps them **digest** their food. Digest means to break down food inside the stomach so the body can use it. The bodies of cold-blooded animals have more energy to digest food faster when they are warmer.

Sometimes it is easy for iguanas to find fruit to eat. This is because of **mast fruiting**. Mast fruiting happens when many trees in a large area produce a lot of fruit at the same time. This happens about every three to seven years. During this time, iguanas eat a lot of fruit. Their body turns the extra fruit into fat and stores it under their jaws and in their neck.

After mast fruiting, there are many months when it is hard to find fruit. During this time, iguanas eat leaves and live off their stored fat.

Marine iguanas eat seaweed from the ocean floor. They can hold their breath for up to one hour. This means that they have time to dive, find food, and eat underwater before coming up for air.

These male iguanas are about to fight each other.

An Iguana's Life Cycle

Iguanas mate at different times of the year. In the rain forest, most iguanas mate just after the rainy season. The rainy season is a period of several months when it rains almost every day. Usually the rainy season is during the fall or early winter.

Males and females may change to brighter colors during the mating season. The bright colors show other iguanas that they are ready to mate.

When a male iguana wants to mate with a female iguana, he may raise his dewlap. When he does this, he is telling other males to get away. A male may charge toward any male that comes too close.

Male iguanas often fight with each other when they both want to mate with the same female. They may scratch, bite, or hit each other with their tail until one of them runs away.

Eggs and Young

After a male and female iguana have mated, the female often lies in the sun for a long time. This warms the eggs inside her. The female carries her eggs for up to two months.

Then, she looks for a sunny spot of soft ground where she can lay her eggs. The eggs need the sun to warm them so they will develop. It is often hard to find a good spot because many areas do not receive enough sun. When this happens, female iguanas may fight each other for good places to lay their eggs.

Before laying eggs, the female digs a hole in the ground with her claws and nose. She lays her eggs in the hole. A female iguana lays up to 50 eggs at a time.

After laying the eggs, the female covers them with soil. The soil helps to protect the eggs from other animals. Sometimes the mother also digs other holes to confuse animals looking for eggs to eat. Once the female iguana covers her eggs with soil, she leaves them. Like many other reptiles, adult iguanas do not take care of their young.

The eggs hatch in eight to ten weeks. Newly hatched iguanas are less than 1 foot (30 cm) long.

These young iguanas are climbing on their mother.

They look like small adult iguanas, but they are a lighter color.

Iguanas never stop growing. They shed their skin as their bodies grow larger. Iguanas shed their skin in small pieces, instead of in one large piece like snakes.

Wild iguanas live from 10 to 15 years. Iguanas in zoos may live up to 20 years.

Surviving in the Rain Forest

Young iguanas are in great danger from predators. Many larger animals of the rain forest will eat young iguanas if they can catch them. Young iguanas are usually bright green with a brown striped tail. These colors camouflage them in the trees. As the iguana gets older, its bright green color often changes to a grayish green or brown. But its belly usually stays bright green.

Iguanas do different things to scare off predators, such as birds and larger lizards. They open their mouth to show their teeth. They may hiss and puff up their body. They bob their head up and down and swish their tail back and forth. Sometimes they raise their front legs to make themselves look larger. If they look larger, there is a better chance that smaller animals will be afraid of them.

Young iguanas live lower in the canopy. There, the leaves grow closer together, and it is easier to hide.

Adult iguanas live higher in the canopy, where it is sunnier. There are good spots for basking there. Bask means to lie under a heat source to raise the body temperature. Adult iguanas sometimes fight each other for the best places to bask.

When they begin their day, iguanas leave their sleeping places and move to a basking site. There, they lie in the sun for several hours. After they are warm, they climb trees and look for food. They then bask again, while their food digests. When night comes, they return to their sleeping places.

In order to survive, green iguanas need rain forest trees to provide food.

The Future of Iguanas

Like many wild animals, iguanas are losing their habitat. The rain forests of Central America are disappearing. People are cutting down trees to make room for new homes and farms. They are also selling the wood from trees. Iguanas cannot survive without the forests.

Iguanas are also the most popular pet lizards in the world today. Traders buy iguanas and sell them as pets. Iguanas need a lot of special attention. Many people do not know how to take care of them. When taken from the wild, iguanas may become sick or die. That is because they need a certain amount of sun and certain temperatures to live. It is hard for people to create the conditions iguanas need in order to survive.

This green iguana is basking in a tree.

 Iguanas can lose their tail and grow a new one. Sometimes an iguana's tail is broken off by a predator. When the new tail grows back, it is usually shorter than the old tail. Most lizards can grow a new tail like this.

What Will Happen to Iguanas?

Some people are raising iguanas on farms. These iguanas are then sold as pets or as food. In this way, wild iguanas are not taken from the rain forest to be pets.

Some countries are trying to save the iguana. They have made laws against catching and selling iguanas as pets. Without laws, the sale and removal of iguanas from their habitats would probably increase.

Laws are not enough. People must make sure that the laws are obeyed. They must report people who break the laws. They must teach other people about the importance of iguanas. Laws and learning may help people keep iguanas alive in their rain forest homes for a very long time.

head
see page 13

eyes
see page 13

dewlap
see page 13

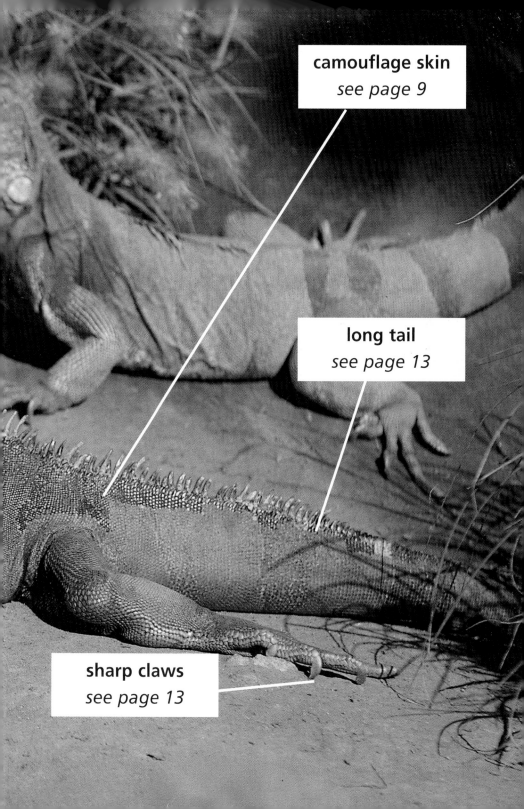

camouflage skin
see page 9

long tail
see page 13

sharp claws
see page 13

Glossary

arboreal (ar-BOR-ee-ul)—living mainly in trees

camouflage (KAM-o-flaj)—colors, shapes, and patterns that make something blend in with its background

canopy (KAN-uh-pee)—a thick area of leaves high up in the treetops

cold-blooded (KOHLD BLUHD-id)—animals with body temperatures that change according to their surroundings

digest (dye-JEST)—to break down food so the body can use it

habitats (HAB-i-tats)—places where an animal or plant usually lives

mast fruiting (MAST FROOT-ing)—when many trees in a large area produce a lot of fruit at the same time

scales (SKAYLS)—small pieces of thick, hard skin

species (SPEE-sees)—a group of animals or plants most closely related to each other in the scientific classification system

territorial (tayr-i-TOR-ee-uhl)—an animal that defends the land it has claimed as its home

Internet Sites

Iguana Spot
www.geocities.com/ig_chick/

Rain Forest Action Network: Kids' Corner
www.ran.org/kids_action

Useful Address

International Iguana Society
P.O. Box 366188
Bonita Springs, FL 34136

Books to Read

Mara, W. P. *Iguanas.* Mankato, MN: Capstone
Press, 1996.

Patton, Don. *Iguanas.* New York: Child's World,
1996.

Index